BIG M:
THE MAMMOTH OF MOORPARK

Painting by Stev H. Ominski©2007 Used with permission.

by

Curtis D. Abdouch

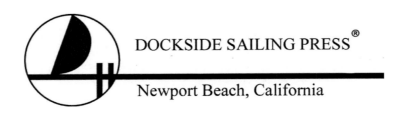

DOCKSIDE SAILING PRESS®

Newport Beach, California

Printed in the United States of America

CONTENTS

INTRODUCTION

This is the story of one animal that met its demise long before a human could have witnessed it. The story is part scientific conjecture based on the evidence uncovered and revealed, but it is mostly true. While the main character is the mammoth itself, you will meet people who helped shape the story, and without whom it would have probably never happened. While you will read about master artists of ancient eras who painted likenesses of animals that surrounded them in their daily lives, cameras, of course, were not around in prehistoric times to record events or anything else. That's why the graphics in this book combine illustrations, photos and maps, all to help bring the story alive and close to you, the reader.

SOMETHING REMARKABLE

Moorpark, California is a small pleasant town in Ventura County not too far from the sea. Moorpark's town center boasts a performing arts theater, retail stores, a nice civic center and restaurants. On Moorpark Avenue, Kahoot's is a large store that promises everything for the horse lover. For this reason, some might have called this community "horse country." But it was about to be called something else.

In 2005, the population of Moorpark was 35,000. It was about to get bigger, because a subdivision up the road and east of the town center promised housing for more future residents.

But this was not the only thing that was about to be big.

On March 29, 2005, life in Moorpark began about the same as any other day. People went about their usual business. City Hall was hosting people seeking building permits or who had other municipal business. Nothing seemed unusual.

Up the road the pre-construction earthmoving machines were carving out the landscape to make it suitable for building homes. But then, something remarkable happened. One of those giant machines upended an object no one expected: the tusk of an elephant. This was no ordinary elephant, not one from the circus, not one from Africa, but one that had come down the "elephant highway"—a migration route—in North America a very long time ago. This elephant was a mammoth, and this was no ordinary mammoth. This was anything but business as usual in Moorpark, California.

Who knew that five-ton prehistoric members of the elephant family used to live in Moorpark's own back yard? And who knew that the life of at least one would end there, leaving all to marvel today at its place in prehistory?

Mammoths and mastodons are no strangers to southern California. Special fossil deposits, like those at the La Brea Tar Pits in the heart of Los Angeles, have given up remains of mammoths over the last century. From time to time, they also have turned up during the extensive urban and suburban development that has occurred over the last several decades in southern California.

Every discovery of a visitor from the past like a mammoth is exciting. But the story—and journey of discovery that occurred in Moorpark in late March and early April 2005—is different and even more important and exciting!

Welcome to Mammoth Country!

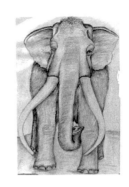

THE LAST LONG JOURNEY

The tracks she stamped in the soft mud were nearly as big as car tires. They measured six feet around, which gave a clue about how big she really was. The giant with the big feet plodded along at a steady pace as long as she could. But the furnace deep inside her demanded fuel, and she was often forced to stop and feed. The bouts of aggressive grazing were so frequent that progress was slow even when attempting an all-out march of eight miles an hour. With those energy demands, her metabolism obliged her to consume nearly 700 pounds of hard-to-digest grasses every day.

As she grazed, the sun briefly warmed the landscape, but had little time to start drying the mud and the numerous puddles and pools that she sloshed through effortlessly mile after mile.

The mammoth's first image of a sabertoothed cat that crossed her path was hazy. But as she came closer, she could focus better as it lay crouched as if ready to ambush something. The big cat's lips wrinkled. Its yellow eyes stared straight at her, and it snarled as it opened its mouth to a 120-degree angle to bare its dagger-like canine teeth. Not about to be stopped or even slowed by the menacing cat, "Her Highness" answered as she blasted a short but convincing note from her trunk. The trumpeting penetrated the air

SABERTOOTHED CAT

sharply and startled the predator from its position without further challenge. Although the cat was no serious threat, her signal and uninterrupted approach clearly showed who was boss. The cat might have had better luck hunting a small group of prehistoric camels nibbling leaves from a grove of trees not far off.

Camels

The camel group of mammals such as the western camel (*Camelops hesternus*) in this story is known collectively as camelids. Camels originated in North America. Even an early species of long-necked llama (*Hemiauchenia macrocephala*) was known to live in the open grasslands of southern California. But all North American camelids became extinct by the end of the last Ice Age 10,000 years ago. Today, however, camels thrive in Asia (the dromedary and the bactrian) and in Africa. South America boasts four different camel species—the llama, the vicuna, the alpaca and the guanaco.

WESTERN CAMEL

A short time and distance later, a herd of lightly striped horses galloped off, kicking at each other as they ran into the hills on her right. She could hear their hooves pounding through the mud and their braying that sounded a bit like zebras or mules, but she could not see them at all.

WESTERN HORSE

Horses

Like the camels, North America was a first home of horses. And like camels, all species became extinct in their homeland, only to be reintroduced to the Americas by European explorers in the 1500s.

In the distance, yet another storm was developing and heading straight for her as she headed cross-country in the direction it was coming. About 16 miles before it reached her, she could smell it, and she could clearly hear the rumble of thunder at that distance as her large ears flapped gently to the rhythm of her walk.

STORM OF DOOM

Rain had been falling for days, here and there and from time to time, making travel difficult for many animals. A family of peccaries she encountered on her journey made the most of the mud, wallowing and playing in it much like their modern pig cousins. But many animals just laid low in whatever precious shelter the landscape afforded them. There was no refuge for an animal of her size, so she went about daily life exposed to whatever elements nature brought her way.

It was not as bad as it seemed. She was well adapted—equipped—for the lifestyle she led. Her speed in a full raging charge that carried her 10,000-pound hulk forward on her pillar-like legs was truly terrifying and unstoppable. Although her eyesight was not the best, her senses of smell and hearing were better than most. In fact not only had she sensed the coming rain, but also the faint odor of gases still lingering in the air from a distant volcano that had belched its contents during a recent eruption.

Four hours later, as she was about to meet the storm head on, the first hints arrived. A preview of light sprinkles greeted the traveler, but they soon gave way to huge drops of crystal clear rain. Moments later she was in the middle of a downpour.

Her skin surface, studded with stiff bristly hairs, was more sensitive than one would imagine of such a large beast. The small rivers that formed in the wrinkles of her thick hide trickled down and bathed away the trail grime that had built up on her body earlier during her journey. The shower felt refreshing.

Thin witch-like fingers of dense fog rose up from the ocean to her left and crept over the cliff to join the torrents of rain from above. She had lost sight of the cliff, but continued to trek north along the soggy path worn bare by fellow travelers over the years. On this day, she was alone.

Although she was drenched, nothing—not the rain, lightning or thunder or fog—slowed her determined progress. Yet she could not know that this was the last day of her life. Standing 12 feet at the shoulder, maybe 14 at the top of her towering head, she was the tallest thing on this bleak stretch of prehistoric coastal landscape.

Just ahead of her lay a pool of muddy water in the middle of the pathway. Although the pool was not wide, the rains had filled a deep depression in the trail. She could not see the bottom through the muck, so she entered it without hesitation. As she waded out she sunk into the mud with such force that the pool engulfed all four legs up to her belly. As she was sucked into the mud and water, her massive bulk displaced the muck, and the level rose to surround more of her body. The mud gripped her legs like a vacuum. It was only then that she found out that the depth had deceived her.

For several hours she plowed and splashed and struggled and wobbled in an effort to break its suction, but the mud held her legs hostage. She thrashed and smacked her trunk against the surface like the crack of a whip and wheeled her head wildly about, looking for something nearby—a rock or a tree perhaps—to wrap her trunk around to winch herself free. There was nothing; she was literally in deep trouble.

All the commotion was bound to attract attention. And it did. Other mammoths heard the distress from long distances and came to investigate. That is all they did. No assistance was forthcoming, as they seemed to understand that there was trouble of which they wanted no part. They just shook their heads from side to side, turned and slowly walked away. Large birds of prey circled overhead, sensing that there soon might be carrion on which to feast. **BIG M** paid no attention to them.

TRAPPED IN THE MUD HOLE
Illustration copyright 2001 Mark Hallett Paleoart. Used with permission.

Sometimes during her hours of struggle against the elements, she tired from all the thrashing about. Then she relaxed. And so did her trunk. When that happened, her trunk lay on the surface of the pool or dipped just below it. Air released through her trunk would create a deep gurgling sound in the muck, and it would bubble much like blowing air through a drinking straw into water or chocolate milk.

Once, for a moment, she freed her left front leg. To have freed another leg—a wrong one—from the mud at nearly the same time might have caused her to lose her balance and topple over and drown. But that did not happen. The mud held her other three legs fast, and she was never able to move. Drowning was a cause of death denied.

A sudden burst of thunder was the last thing she ever heard. The sound seemed to fill the space between every molecule of air within a mile of her. She bellowed in intense startled pain. A bolt of lightning had struck her straight on, splitting her skull. The tremendous shock traveled through her body burning flesh along the way. The water that surrounded her completed her electrocution. In that moment of final pain, she heaved forward and even appeared to leap, a feat that is physically impossible for elephants.

The force of the terrible shock caused her legs to buckle instead. At the next moment, she did indeed topple over. As she fell over, the huge splash nearly drained the pool. Her lifeless body lay on its side, taking up most of the muddy hole. She had created her own grave. For that one brief, fatal moment, water and electricity had conspired to cause her instant death. Once was enough.

In the final analysis, the burned flesh would decompose more quickly. The mud and water mixture closed in around her, sealing her grave. Silence settled over the area, except for the relentless pelting of rain.

Perhaps it was just as well that the elder lady's life had ended suddenly. After all, she was approximately 50 to 55 years old. In the succession of six sets of teeth that she and her kind grew and replaced during their lifetimes, the crowns of her final set had begun to wear smooth. Grinding the tough grasses that made up her diet would have become increasingly difficult. Finally her teeth would have lost their grinding capacity altogether. When that happened, she would become unable to eat effectively, and she would be doomed to a slow and agonizing death by starvation.

Hers was but one life removed from the tapestry of the population and the species. But it had been an important one in the natural order of things on the planet nearly a million years younger than now. Her modern relatives, as well as early humankind would not appear on the stage of prehistoric life in this area for another several hundred thousand years.

BIG M's POST MORTEM

The odor of burned skin, bone, hair and brain had quickly dissolved in the rain. As if in tribute to Her Highness, the storm, for a moment, gave up its attack. As her soaked carcass lay in the stillness of the pool, mud flowed into the long nostrils of her trunk, clogging the lifeless tunnels. Mud oozed into her partially open mouth in amounts that would have gagged her, but there was no such reflex. Her body also had formed a kind of dam and soon the mud began to well up and deepen along her back. When the storm resumed its daily rage and ravage, the mud eroding from the steep slope in front of her finally topped the dam and covered most of her lifeless mass until there was little more than a peep here and there of a body showing at all.

The form had grown into a soft muddy mound that protected the carcass and deprived opportunistic predators and snooping scavengers of their next feast. The rains had been so heavy that even airborne scavengers such as vultures that could have landed on her carcass and picked away at it, did not arrive on the scene. It had not been good flying weather. The birds had been grounded miles away to wait out the storms in a sheltered roost.

By the time they were able to resume their aerial surveys, even those that circled the site could not detect a body. Their acute telescopic eyes detected only a muddy mound on the quiet landscape below.

Even though larger animals were denied nourishment, the subsurface worms, microbes, scavenging insects and their larvae worked around the clock to liberate the tons of rotting meat from the framework of bones and teeth. The ground never froze, the sun finally broke, the pool dried up and the heat baked the mound solid. The volume of flesh disappeared, due largely to the excavation and demolition work of the decomposers inside the carcass. With the mass lost, the mound cracked and slumped from its own weight.

Months later, the skeleton was fully free of flesh and organs, but still encased in the mound. No eyes, no trunk, no tail, no tongue remained, all atoms of which by now had been contributed and consigned to life in the future.

The mud deposited in the first season would be repeated for the next several centuries, then millennia, as the rains buried the skeleton under tons more mud. Pressure and minerals finally turned the muddy sediments and bone to rock, and a fossil was all that remained of **BIG M**.

DAY OF DISCOVERY

O n a warm spring day, March 29, 2005 to be exact, Trevor Lindsey, a professional paleontologist (an expert in prehistoric life) was monitoring a site being graded for the future site of a 265-home community known as Meridian Hills, just northeast of Moorpark, California. Diesel exhaust blew out of the stacks of huge earth-moving machines as they slowly carved and transformed an area in the foothills where the new homes eventually would be built. The site was owned and being prepared for development by the William Lyons Company in Calabasas, California.

A law required the developer to hire a professional of Trevor's background and expertise to be there in case fossils or human artifacts were found. This kind of monitoring is done as part of Moorpark's development requirements, just in case something old, ancient or even prehistoric is found. Something like the remains of an Indian settlement perhaps. Or a mammoth skeleton. Who knows what might turn up?

More often than not, this kind of monitoring does not yield much, maybe some old bottles or some old horse or cattle bones. But just in case, monitors are there. As the law required him to do, Trevor followed the machines as they growled like lions relentlessly across the landscape.

It was a good thing on March 29, when an earthmover operator reported that he had struck something suspicious—something that looked as if it could be a bone. Trevor quickly reached the location and began to investigate. As other big machines continued their relentless carving of the landscape all around, the monitor kneeled down and brushed aside the dirt for a closer look. What he saw surprised him. Sure enough, it was a fossil. For a while, he probed and dug carefully not to damage the specimen and to try to find out if there was more. There was. He was now looking at a piece of tusk—a mammoth tusk! And there was a lot more. Trevor ordered all work to be stopped. In the middle of the 325-acre Meridian Hills development was a mammoth skeleton!

Just how much of the skeleton was there was not known, but it was probably more than one person could handle responsibly. Realizing that it would be too big a job to dig the mammoth's remains out himself, Trevor called for backup.

When the hastily assembled reinforcements arrived on the scene on April 1, the team was comprised of more paleontologists, mapping experts and excavators. They were well prepared to do a good job, and do it in a hurry.

As far as the public was concerned, the first hint that something big had broken—besides a mammoth tusk—was a phone call that Moorpark Assistant City Manager and Public Information Officer Hugh Riley received. He was told that media trucks were converging in Meridian Hills and that he'd better leave the office in City Hall to investigate. Once there, he was confronted not only by a swarm of anxious news teams, but a whole new situation he was hardly prepared to deal with. But Hugh was a quick and eager learner, and he knew that this story was going to be important to the community. It did not take him long to figure out that just like a mammoth itself, there was a BIG story to be told here, and he was the person who was going to tell it.

HUGH RILEY, MOORPARK ASSISTANT CITY MANAGER

For the next several days, the breaking story of a mammoth uncovered after centuries—or possibly millennia—was gripping the local residents. Even national news media came calling and was busy capturing the excavation. Each and every member of the media was greeted and treated to quite an unusual story. After all, even in mammoth country, one didn't find a mammoth every day.

With cameras rolling and reporters looking on, the media focused on the excavation team's methodical work. For their part, with tools ranging from jackhammers to dental picks, members of the team carefully, yet excitedly removed bone after bone of the massive fossilized skeleton and wrapped them in plaster jackets. For long hours, then days, the experts labored to make sure the mammoth would be free again. It was hot, dirty, but exciting work. Every bone, tooth, tusk and other fossil fragment had to be photographed and mapped before it was removed from its location in the ground. Most of the days were sunny, about 90 degrees Fahrenheit. "It was definitely lemonade weather," remarked Mark Roeder, the chief excavator, as he wiped sweat from his forehead.

THE CAREFUL PROCESS OF EXCAVATION. PALEONTOLOGIST AND CHIEF EXCAVATOR, MARK ROEDER, IS IN THE BACKGROUND

On April 8, the team completed its excavation work, and on April 9, they returned to protect and prepare the fossils for the trip to the lab. By wrapping the fossils with layers of newspaper, burlap cloth and aluminum foil and finally covering them in a jacket of plaster, the team accomplished the task. The work was similar to the way a doctor puts a cast on a broken arm or leg. This protected the fossilized bones from being damaged when loaded onto a truck.

After nine scorching days of labor, the team recovered a remarkable 75% of the mammoth's remains, and they were transported off the site to the lab for analysis. The excavation team also removed about 6,000 pounds of soil that immediately surrounded **BIG M's** resting place. **BIG M** was free again, free at long last.

> ### 5 April
> I arrived at the site at 6:30 AM. I have Aaron Biehl measure a section from the site up the hill to the top of the cut. Also Aaron mapped the micro stratigraphy of the site. We had visitors from Wm. Lyons Homes and the City of Moorpark. Trevor Lindsey was by several times.
>
> We jacketed the following specimen: scapula TJL032805-U. We pulled the following specimens: jaw frag/tooth TJL032805-I, humerus end frag TJL032805-K, rib fragment TJL032805-W, rib fragments TJL032805-Xj, Xi, and lower jaw fragment TJL032805-AA.
>
> We left at 6:00 PM.

SAMPLE OF MARK ROEDER'S FIELD NOTES

SKILLED VOLUNTEERS PLAY A VITAL ROLE

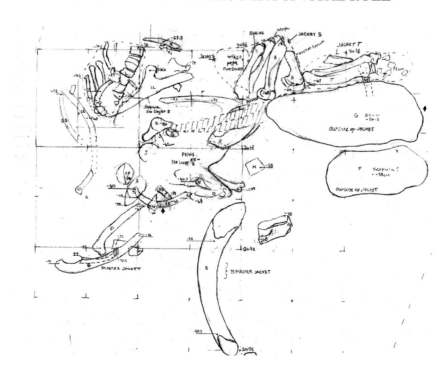

A HAND-DRAWN MAP RECORDED BONE POSITIONS BEFORE REMOVAL

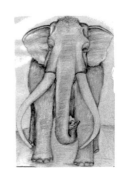

BIG M's UNSOLVED MYSTERIES

Even though **BIG M** was no longer surrounded by soil, she was still surrounded in another way—by mystery. Though there was no crime and no victim of foul play, there were many unanswered questions. Now came the investigation.

Just as modern day detectives search for clues, so do scientists, who search for answers to more questions than probably can be answered. Scientists who studied the Moorpark fossil relied on the bones and other remains to tell them—and us—a lot about the mammoth. The bones speak; the scientists listen and learn.

Was **BIG M** a male or female? What kind of mammoth was it? From what point in geologic time might it have lived, and what was its age when it died? Here is what experts thought they knew.

- Species: It was first thought to be a southern mammoth, *Archidiskodon meridionalis,* a species far older than the more recent and common mammoths that also lived in North America. Unlike its woolly and Columbian mammoth cousins, the southern mammoth pre-dates human presence on the continent as well. At the time of this story, *Archidiskodon* was the first part of the scientific name of the species to which **BIG M** belonged. But the name has changed and the southern mammoth is now recognized by scientists as *Mammuthus meridionalis*.

- Although few individuals of this species have been found in the U.S., experts believe that there was a rather substantial population. They also believe that the animals lived in herds, much like African elephants live on the savannah today.
- Geologic time period: Pleistocene Epoch, which included the last Ice Age. Southern mammoths were the first to enter North America from Asia about 1.4 million years ago.
- Gender: Female.
- Age: Between 50 and 55 years old, as told by the teeth.
- Size: 12 feet tall at the shoulder, probably 5 tons or more.

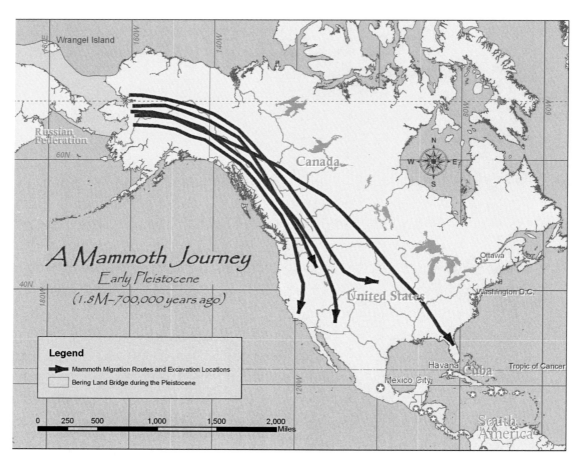

Bering Land Bridge

The land "bridge" over the Bering Sea had already formed when **BIG M** and her kind crossed over into North America from Asia over one million years ago. The sea level at the Bering Strait (and many other places) had dropped due to vast amounts of liquid seawater freezing and being stored as ice during the Pleistocene Epoch (the last Ice Age). The "bridge" was dry land— actually the exposed floor of the Bering Sea and not really a structure built *over* the water as one thinks of a bridge. It was thought to be about 500 to 600 miles wide measuring from north to south. At its maximum, the bridge measured as much as 1,000 miles wide from north to south and as much as 3,000 miles long from west to east.

The land bridge was a "two-way street" allowing mammoths, humans and others to come into North America and giving passage to camels and horses that were migrating out of the continent.

This was the route that **BIG M**—as well as all other mammoth species—took to this continent. However, thousands of years later, humans crossing from Siberia in Asia to Alaska in North America were stopped cold in their tracks because huge glaciers blocked their way forward. Having their passage to North America interrupted had severe consequences. They were forced to settle on the land bridge itself, which became a sort of prehistoric country known as Beringia. According to varying estimates, the settlement lasted from 10,000 to as long as 22,000 years, so this was no minor camp-out on the way to a new world.

As a female why was she alone? Did her companions sense trouble and avoid the mud hole? After all, most female elephants live together in closely bonded groups, caring for young and youthful members of the herd. An older experienced female known as a matriarch leads the herd. Was **BIG M** a former matriarch on a lonely death march? Why was she where she was when her life ended? The scientists have no answers for these questions.

An Ice Age Riddle

There is no doubt that the southern mammoth, **BIG M's** kind, crossed into North America by way of the Bering Land Bridge. The *southern* mammoth was so named because it was a subtropical to tropical species. So how and when did these warm-climate mammoths cross the Bering Land Bridge without freezing to death?

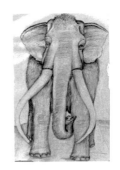

MAMMOTHS, MATRIX AND MICROFOSSILS

Did **BIG M** have company after her death? Other than the post mortem dinner party she hosted for the numerous microorganisms and other decomposers, were there other "dirty little secrets" hidden away too?

In the past, when a fossil like **BIG M** was found, the main attractions were the bones. Not much else mattered or was preserved by scientists and other fossil hunters. More recently, paleontologists and archaeologists realized that smaller specimens told their own important stories about diet, climate and the condition of the habitat and ecosystem. Scientists now eagerly and patiently sort out these microfossils—teeth, claws, hair and tiny bones of other animals, as well as pollen grains, grass and leaf fragments, parts of insects, even animal droppings. They are collected from sediments—soil, sand, gravel and ash—known as matrix.

From the world-famous Page Museum at the La Brea Tar Pits in Los Angeles, to Cornell University in New York, microfossils have huge importance. At the Page Museum, workers sort through matrix from tar pit excavations day after day. They find claws, snail shells, grass and leaf fragments, tiny bones, teeth and insects. Not only have scientists learned what the local area was like as long ago as 40,000 years, they have even discovered new forms of life that might have remained completely unknown had it not been for the matrix.

The matrix in New York is different. Not only are the contents different, so was an animal, in this case a mastodon. At Cornell, Professor John Chiment, who led the excavation in 1999, wanted students around the world to participate in a real scientific project. So he mailed out five-pound bags of matrix for them to sort and send back to the lab. The students found seeds, wood, cones from spruce trees, chips of ivory mastodon tusks, insects, hair and other microfossils. All came from the excavation of the specimen known as the Gilbert mastodon.

That's why 6,000 pounds of soil were collected and transported to the lab along with **BIG M**. In that matrix, smaller fossils of other animals that might have lived in her prehistoric neighborhood might be found. In this case, the microfossils told far more about this animal than could have been predicted.

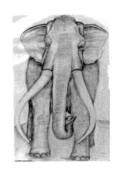

THE MINI BUT MIGHTY

Voles are small rodents that belong to a group or *"genus"* of mammals. Voles belong to the genus *Microtus*, and the various species within the group are called *microtene*s. Modern voles are sometimes referred to as meadow mice. They are mouse-size with small beady eyes. Their remains and the remains of their cousins such as rats, mice and gophers are quite often found in the matrix that surrounds the bones of a larger specimen such as a mammoth. Several months after **BIG M's** excavation, the matrix was about to be cleaned and analyzed. The outcome of this process is never certain; excavators predicted that this batch would not contain many microfossils. But what it lacked in number it made up for in importance.

Washing 6,000 pounds of dirt through a series of filters was a long process. After it was washed it had to dry before experts could sort through it and separate the small fossil material from the sediment waste. The microfossils the experts collected, as predicted, did not contain much. Only a few gopher teeth and a single tooth from a prehistoric *microtene* were recovered. But when the teeth were examined by other experts, they discovered that this particular *microtene* tooth belonged to a species that had died out about 800,000 years ago. No other mammoth lived and died that long ago except one kind: the southern mammoth.

Had this little vole-like rodent lived more recently, say about the same time as Woolly or Columbian mammoths did, the tooth would not have been located in the same layer of rock and soil as **BIG M's** remains. Then the identity of this mammoth might have remained controversial. But a single tooth told the truth, just as evidence would in a good detective story. The conclusion that **BIG M** was a southern mammoth was much more certain now. It was a case in which a tiny rodent fossil made a huge impact on the outcome of a mammoth story. Just think about the chance of finding one tiny tooth in 6,000 pounds of dirt, and this result is even more remarkable!

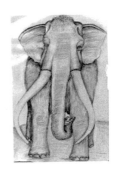

A LONG CURVED PUZZLE

Moorpark had its mammoth. Simi Valley, the first town to the east, was home to the Reagan Presidential Library. And just beyond lay the town of Chatsworth. To museum professionals around the world, at that time Chatsworth was known for Valley Anatomical Preparations. Valley Anatomical was famous in the museum world for two reasons: for supplying museum-quality, animal-related replicas for museum exhibits, education programs and even for home décor from time to time. The other quality for which the company was well known and respected was its ability to acquire original specimens from around the world and the rights to replicate them. Most of these replicas came in the form of bones, skulls, some cultural/archaeological artifacts, complete skeletons of many species and a few scale models of prehistoric animals.

The City of Moorpark had a need. It needed a small-scale traveling exhibit for festivals, school visits and other events in which it could tell the mammoth story. Valley Anatomical was the place to go. The owner and director of operations was Mary Odano. Mary was technically very hands-on, and Valley Anatomical's extensive inventory of specimens was able to supply exhibit components such as a complete sabertoothed cat skull and a mammoth footprint without a problem.

The Valley Anatomical staff also was asked to make replicas of several of **BIG M's** well-preserved teeth and a foot that had most of the bones preserved too. That was relatively easy to carry out as well, although it entailed custom work.

Although Mary and her staff were very good at what they did, the Moorpark project presented a puzzle of unusual twists and curves.

Elephant tusks are really elongated teeth. They are used to move objects and used for defense and aggression against enemies. Mammoth tusks from various species have peculiar twists and curves. Woolly mammoth tusks are different from those of Columbian or southern mammoths. And those in turn are different from modern African or Asian elephants. So just how would an incomplete southern mammoth tusk from **BIG M** be replicated from the broken parts that were brought to Valley Anatomical? To complicate matters, some sections of the long tusk were completely missing.

To uncomplicate matters, Mary and her staff went to work assembling pieces they did have into some kind of order. Measurements of circumference and diameter were taken. From those measurements they could figure the size of the missing piece. That turned out to be a section about three feet long. Her staff was able to sculpt the missing piece so that it fit perfectly along the length of the tusk. After several days, the Valley Anatomical staff was able to assemble the broken pieces in the order that they had grown originally, along with the artificial material for the part of the tusk that was missing. They made a mold of the tusk and, from that, made a full-size replica called a cast. When the work was complete, the tusk measured a full nine feet along its twists and curves. Quite a tooth indeed!

THE AUTHOR WITH THE REPRODUCTION OF **BIG M'S** TUSK

Traveling back west to Simi Valley, another surprise for Moorpark was waiting. Located there was the studio and shop of Animal Makers, Inc. Owned and operated by Jim and Crystal Boulden, this company was famous for full-scale animal models, some modern, some prehistoric, most very realistic, but also some in the realm of pure fantasy. Their clients were the major Hollywood movie studios and producers of television commercials in which animal models appeared.

Animal Makers supplied Moorpark with a true-to-life, small–scale model, called a *maquette*, of the Moorpark mammoth. This made the Moorpark exhibit complete. Today the maquette resides in the Moorpark City Hall.

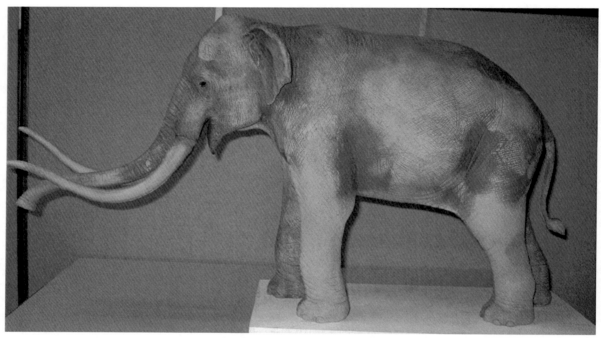

THE MAQUETTE OF **BIG M**

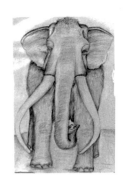

FAMOUS FOSSILS: WHAT'S IN A NAME?

People like to name things. They give all kinds of names to all kinds of things. They think names give things more personal identity. They can form closer bonds with things that have names. Think of your own pet. Chances are you don't simply call it dog, cat, bird, lizard or fish.

Scientists name species of plants and animals so they have references to them when they communicate with each other about an organism. Sometimes part of the scientific name refers to the person who discovered the original specimen of the species. It might be named in honor of someone or the location of the specimen when it was found. Often the name describes a particular characteristic or structure of the organism, such a particular kind of wing, tooth, head, foot, leaf or petal. Sometimes even scientific names change. As scientists acquire more specimens for study and see where they fit in the fossil record, the original identification can be changed to reflect the results of ongoing study and new knowledge. All life forms have a two-part name. The first name is its "generic" name to specify the group or genus to which it belongs. The genus is always capitalized. The second or last name is the "specific" name and refers to the species. It is always spelled with small letters. It is also proper to print the name in italics.

As mentioned previously, **BIG M's** scientific name now is *Mammuthus meridionalis*. No matter where in the world scientists are located, they all know that *Mammuthus meridionalis* is one specific kind of mammoth and not another. (Coincidently, prior to **BIG M's** discovery, the developer of the land had named the future community "Meridian Hills".)

The Gilbert mastodon mentioned earlier isn't a mammoth. But this specimen was given a name too. Many other mammoths have become famous, and they have also been named or recognized in some outstanding way. Mammoths have been found on many continents and countries around the world, especially in Europe, Asia and North America. Their remains have been found in nearly every state in the nation and even as far south as Central America!

The last place on earth where mammoths lived was an island in the Arctic Ocean. Their remains were found on Wrangel Island, and there is a surprise. They were dwarf woolly mammoths, much smaller than their huge relatives of earlier times. This population of Wrangel Island dwarfs was still alive off the coast of Russia until about 3,800 years ago. By then, the great pyramids in the Egyptian desert already had been built!

Head south along the coast of the Pacific Ocean, and Santa Rosa Island will come into view. That is where another population of dwarf mammoths lived until they too became extinct. These were Columbian mammoths. Experts think that winds blowing from west to east carried the scent of vegetation they wanted for food. So they swam across the channel—probably about 20 miles—to get it. When they arrived on the island, they found what they were looking for. But they could not smell their home back on the mainland coast of California, because the winds on the island were blowing the scent of the mainland away from them. The mammoths became stranded on the island and these castaways lived out on the island for thousands of years. The space and the amount of food on the island was reduced, so, in response to fewer resources, over many generations, their size was reduced as well. Today, the skeletons of these mammoths are on exhibit at the Channel Islands National Park.

Twenty nine individuals of the 33 mammoths found at the La Brea Tar Pits in Los Angeles, California came from the excavation of just one pit: Pit 9. They are estimated to be about 40,000 years old—among the oldest of the specimens in the museum's Ice Age collection, the largest in the world. The Pit 9 mammoths seem to be juveniles, but why they were all together in that one pit is a mystery. Woolly mammoths did not venture south into California, but the Columbians did. All mammoths at La Brea are Columbian.

Traveling inland in the United States introduces two states that have impressive records of mammoths. Hot Springs, South Dakota is a famous site in which woolly and Columbian mammoths met their death in a sinkhole.

Nebraska is wonderful place to find mammoths too. There, experts think that as many as 10 mammoths are buried beneath nearly every square mile of landscape in all 93 counties of the state! Mammoths were so numerous that one became the Nebraska State Fossil in 1967. It was collected in 1922 from the Henry Kariger Ranch in Lincoln County, Nebraska and is one of the largest mammoths ever found in the world. According to one report, the mammoth nicknamed "Archie—The World's Largest Elephant," once roamed the hills and drank from the waters of Medicine Creek in southwest Nebraska."

This mammoth was named Archie originally, because, at the time, it was identified and classified as an *Archidiskodon*. But this specimen, found in Lincoln County, Nebraska, was not

Archidiskodon meridionalis, but *Archidiskodon maibeni*, named in honor of Hector Maiben, a farmer from Palmyra, Nebraska, who helped sponsor the expedition and excavation. Over time, the scientific name of this mammoth species was changed to *Elephas maibeni*. Today it stands tall in Morrill Hall, the Nebraska State Museum in Lincoln.

Most of the time, only the harder materials—the bones, tusks and teeth—remain as evidence of mammoths. However, in Russia, there are two famous exceptions. The first one was only a baby. Known as Dima, he was in very poor health and less than a year old when he died and froze in Siberia nearly 40,000 years ago. Yet this three-foot baby still had skin and organs that scientists studied to find out about the relationship between prehistoric and modern elephants. Dima's carcass is now in a museum in St. Petersburg, Russia.

Dima was discovered in 1977. Twenty years later, another discovery sent mammoth shock waves around the world. Location: Siberia. Native Dolgon reindeer herders found huge tusks jutting from the permanently frozen ground. Tusks are usually prized for making tools and for trading for money. But these tusks were gateways to an entire adult carcass, which would prove to be the subject of an incredible and controversial scientific journey.

A French anthropologist and explorer, Bernard Buigues, was looking for just such a prize when one of the Dolgon families led him to this mammoth. Buigues knew this was the frozen treasure he'd been seeking for years. He made a deal with the Dolgons to take possession of it. He named it after them, the now-famous Jarkov mammoth, a woolly mammoth.

The project Buigues had in mind had never been attempted before. His goal was to try to bring mammoths back to life by "cloning." He and other scientists wanted to see if it was possible to restore a long-extinct species to a place alongside animals living on the planet today.

In 1999, in a feat of mammoth proportions, the Jarkov mammoth was freed from the ice, complete with its fur coat and body intact and was flown to an ice cave 60 miles away. There, scientists went to work to recover DNA for the cloning experiments.

Cloning

Clones are organisms that are exact genetic copies. Every single bit of their DNA is identical. Cloning can happen naturally. (Think identical twins.) Or, they can be made in the laboratory. (Think Dolly the sheep.)

Identical twins develop and are born from a single fertile egg from their mother. They are alike in all respects except for their fingerprints.

Dolly the sheep was a biological and media sensation when she appeared in 1997. As the first mammal to be cloned in the lab from an adult cell, she is by far the world's most famous clone.

But it's one thing to clone an animal whose kind is alive today and another to clone an animal that's extinct. (Think mammoth.)

The Jarkov mammoth was the first attempt to bring back a mammoth from extinction. In the late 1990s, it was a noble attempt, but it failed. The research team failed to find even one intact mammoth cell from which DNA might have been extracted. Even the frozen condition of an animal that was 20,300 years old could not preserve the required genetic material for cloning.

MAMMOTH GENOME PROJECT TEAM MEMBER IN DNA LAB

Advances in time and technology led a team of scientists in 2008 at Pennsylvania State University to succeed in sequencing the genome of an extinct animal. The animal was a woolly mammoth, and a genome is an organism's complete set of genetic information. Using highly sophisticated DNA-sequencing instruments that read ancient DNA very efficiently, the team was able to sequence 4.7 billion DNA nucleic acids that make up the mammoth's genetic code or blueprint.

Despite recent advances in DNA-related technology, most experts believe that bringing back any extinct organism will likely not happen. While they see the value in the scientific experiments, they believe the experiments hold little interest for the general public. Fortunately or unfortunately we will probably not see any baby mammoths running around again.

Or will we?

That was the verdict back a few years. A big cloud of doubt. But in 2013, a group of Russian scientists found a "fresh" mammoth carcass on a remote island off the coast of Siberia. It was so fresh that blood seeped from its body and the meat was so tempting that one scientist actually tasted it!

Like **BIG M,** it was female in her mid-fifties, and the scientific team named her Buttercup.

Buttercup is giving up a lot of secrets about her life and death. The hunt continues for the "Holy Grail" of material that can be used to make it possible to cross back over from a state of extinction to the land of the living. Like the permafrost in some northern locations, doubt is beginning to melt. Scientists are still very skeptical, but some are beginning to feel optimistic that the mammoth or at least some other extinct organism will again have a future, not just a past.

MAMMOTHS AND MUD HOLES

Of all the mammoth-related tales in the previous chapter, the story of these two mammoths stands out. They are related because they are both mammoths. They are related because both are female. They are related by cause of death. They are separated by time and distance. One lived and died in Siberia, the other in California. Lyuba was the young Siberian; **BIG M** was the old Californian.

Lyuba's remains were found in the Russian arctic in 2007 by a Nenets reindeer breeder and hunter named Yuri Khudi. He was with his two sons when they found the baby. Although he knew the importance of the discovery, he did not touch the carcass. Nenets tribespeople believe that touching a mammoth carcass is a very bad omen.

Instead, Yuri traveled to a small town miles away to talk with a friend who he thought might be able to help. Together they contacted the director of a local museum who agreed to return to the site of the discovery.

When they arrived at the site, they were surprised to find no baby mammoth carcass. What had happened to it? How did it just disappear? They were worried that some people who wanted to sell the specimen had stolen it. The mystery was solved when they discovered that Yuri's own cousin had taken it to town where he traded it to a store owner for two snowmobiles. The store owner had gone into the museum exhibit business by displaying the remains to attract customers and visitors. Police were able to help rescue Lyuba and move it to the Shemanovsky Museum in Salekhard. The grateful museum officials named the baby Lyuba, which in Russian is the word for love.

Lyuba's body was transferred to Jikei University School of Medicine in Japan for intense but careful and respectful study. The team of researchers at the university used several methods to learn about the baby. For example they used computer tomography scans. A computer tomography (CT) scan is an imaging method that uses x-rays to create pictures of cross-sections of the body. Through this method and other procedures, the team discovered pollen and her mother's milk in her stomach and waste material in her intestine. All signs of a baby in good health. She was likely born in the spring.

She is by far the best preserved mammoth mummy in the world, surpassing Dima, a male mammoth calf mummy which had previously been the best known specimen. (Dima's story is in the previous chapter entitled "Famous Fossils: What's in a Name?")

Indications are that Lyuba died during a river crossing when the river during the spring thaw would have run heavy with sediment. There is a slight conflicting report that she died in a mud hole. It's hard to tell exactly what happened on a particular day 42,000 years ago. In either case there was no mistake: It was death by mud.

Mud helped kill **BIG M** too. Had she not gotten stuck in it, things might have turned out differently. Even without the lightning strike that killed her, it is possible that she might have freed herself after a period of intense struggle against the suction of the mud and had gone ahead with her life in time and distance. Or she might have struggled for days to free herself, only to become exhausted. With exhaustion combined with starvation not far behind, she might have faced a less-than-desirable fate.

But it is hard, even with intelligent guessing, to know what really happened on a particular day 800,000 years ago.

Summary of Known Mammoths Whose Death Was Partially or Entirely Caused by Mud

Little Lyuba	BIG M
Gender: Female	Gender: Female
Species: Woolly mammoth	Species: Southern mammoth
Age: Baby estimated to 30-35 days old	Age: Fully mature, estimated to be 50-55 years old, maybe older
Condition at time of death: Healthy	Condition at time of death: Healthy
Statistics: Approximate height, and weight at time of death: 33 inches tall, 110 pounds	Statistics: Approximate height, and weight at time of death: 12 feet tall, 10,000 pounds
Location: Russia	Location: California
Died: 42,000 years ago	Died: 800,000 years ago
Cause of death: Choked or inhaled and suffocated on mud in a mud hole or while swimming across a muddy river	Cause of death: Got stuck in a mud hole and then was struck by lightning
Condition when found: A nearly perfect mummy with all skin intact on the carcass	Condition when found: A nearly full skeleton about 75 % complete
Final or permanent location of the specimen: Shemanovsky Museum	Final or permanent location of the specimen: Santa Barbara Museum of Natural History

MAMMOTHS AND MANKIND

In the dimmest of lights powered by burning animal fat, a prehistoric human squeezed through a narrow passage to get to his art gallery. Once inside, he lit grass tipped torches that also had been coated with animal fat to keep them burning longer. There, on the walls of a cool cave in Europe were beautiful paintings of Ice Age animals. Bison, horses and bulls galloped across the walls. Wild deer, goats known as ibex and woolly rhinos stood out in their black, red and yellow coats.

This master artist of the Ice Age dipped a large brush made of animal hair into paint made from clay and other mineral and plant pigments. He boldly stroked the wall to make the first line of his newest creation, another animal that was part of his confined world: a mammoth.

Early humans confronted all of these animals and others on a day-to-day basis. Not only did they paint their portraits, but they also hunted them for food. They used their fur and hides for clothing and bedding and bones for tools and building materials. In turn, some, like cave bears and cave lions, hunted them. Mammoth hunting was also dangerous. Groups of hunters needed to get so close to the beasts to throw spears that it was easy to get trampled in a charge or thrown about and battered by a blow from a heavy trunk or long curved tusk.

As more and more caves and their works of art were discovered and studied, experts began to notice changes in the kind and number of images. There were fewer and fewer mammoths and other animals as hunters became more skilled and their weapons improved. Finally mammoths and other Ice Age animals disappeared on both cave walls and the landscape itself altogether. The Ice Age was coming to an end; a mass extinction had begun.

CRO-MAGNON ARTISTS IN FONT DE GAUME CAVE, FRANCE
(Artist: Charles R. Knight, 1920, Wikipedia)

We cannot be sure why these ancestors painted the animals. It may have been for spiritual reasons as much as artistic ones. Timeless and elegant, paintings on cave walls and rock faces were perhaps the first ways in which humans communicated by sharing ideas and information with others.

People today are as impressed and fascinated with mammoths as our early human ancestors were 25,000 years ago. Tusks and bones are still being found and still used to make beautiful carvings and ornaments. Some mammoth remains still support the lives of people of the North in much the same way they supported our early ancestors.

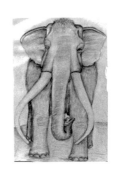

FOR THE RECORD

The fossil record is not a single document stored somewhere for us to refer to. It is the total amount of knowledge we have about the earth's living past. The fossil record of the earth is much larger than it was a century ago, but much smaller than it probably will be 100 years from now. Every day new discoveries are made and added. Sometimes new information replaces old, outdated or even incorrect information. Yet, this record probably will never be complete.

The planet has no capacity to care about the passage of one population or species into extinction. Even huge mass extinctions, which have occurred a few times in earth's history, have not extinguished all life. For life itself is so abundant, so vibrant and so diverse that it acts as its own safety net to survival for those forms that remain and those that arise.

Experts report that life on earth is experiencing another mass extinction. Species are disappearing at a much more rapid and alarming rate than in the past. The cause for much of this is human activity, through pollution, habitat loss, climate change and other factors. The rate of extinction is so rapid in some parts of the world, scientists believe that species are lost even before they can be discovered and described by science, let alone preserved.

All life forms large and small will pass into extinction at some point in time by the forces of the natural world. Humans need to care for their surroundings in a way that will sustain life. It is important to understand that even an individual plant or animal can and does make a contribution and difference, and each one should be valued and respected for its place on the planet.

BIG M: HOME AT LAST

This is not the end of the story, but a new beginning. Having no other choice at the time of excavation, the City of Moorpark took ownership of the fossil bones. They would end up in Mark Roeder's lab and warehouse in Santa Ana until the analysis of the specimen could be completed. There was no museum in Orange County that could house such a specimen. Los Angeles and the world famous Page Museum at the La Brea Tar Pits certainly was in the neighborhood, but it already had the remains of 33 individual Columbian mammoths in its collection. The Santa Barbara Museum of Natural History was also in the area, and was even closer to Moorpark. And it already had a dwarf Columbian mammoth from the Channel Islands on exhibit.

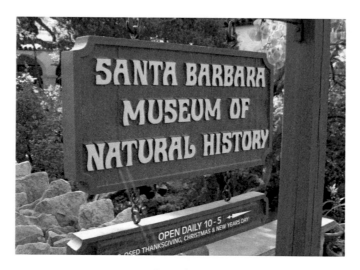

After a series of discussions an agreement was reached: the City of Moorpark would transfer ownership of **BIG M's** remains to the Santa Barbara Museum of Natural History. In turn, the museum would prepare the specimen for exhibition.

The next task was to transfer the fossils from the paleontology lab in Santa Ana to the museum in Santa Barbara. **BIG M's** fragile fossils would travel over two hours and over 125 miles on their final journey.

As for the journey itself, the words "mammoth" and "delicate" usually don't exactly go together in the same thought. But this transfer was actually quite a delicate operation, because these fossils were nearly one million years old. So what better company to handle this trip? None other than Mammoth Moving and Storage located right in Santa Barbara!

MAMMOTH MOVERS

Today the Santa Barbara Museum of Natural History has one of **BIG M's** feet on display as well as one of her molars. The rest of her skeleton has been carefully preserved until the museum has the necessary resources to create a display large enough and suitable for her majesty, **BIG M**.

BIG M'S FOOT BONES

BIG M'S WELL-WORN MOLAR

ECOLOG

This section is usually called an epilogue. An epilogue is a section at the end of a book that serves as a comment on what happened in the story. But this section is called an "Ecolog," because the plight of modern elephants where they live today certainly deserves a comment. The book would not fulfill its purpose without a responsible response to what is happening to the mammoths' cousins now.

In the times of mammoths, early humans were known to hunt or scavenge them. Some believe that these early hunters were at least partially responsible for the extinction of mammoth species, particularly the woolly and the Columbian. There were most likely other factors at play. Some believe that disease and climate change also conspired to bring about extinctions.

Archaeologists have excavated the remains of mammoths that were used to help support the structures of huts and lodges. In these cases, such parts as skins and tusks were used. Undoubtedly, early human families and tribes people prized the massive amounts of meat from a mammoth. It was an excellent source of protein that people needed for survival. Little of the mammoth went to waste; it was too valuable.

Today, if one finds mammoth tusks—and they are found for sure—they can be legally and fairly traded for their valuable ivory. But today's modern elephants—those in Asia and especially Africa—are being hunted to extinction by the greed and unfounded beliefs of people. It is against the law to buy and sell ivory from elephants living today. The elephants, in this case, pay the ultimate price for their elongated teeth. Only the tusks are taken by a sophisticated industry of poachers and black market traders who sell them to some people who believe that ivory holds special powers to those who own the material. The rest of the elephant carcass is left to rot on the blood-soaked ground where the animal was killed. Not only are individuals being killed, but entire herds are slaughtered for this illegal—and immoral—activity.

It might be unpleasant to think about such things as mass elephant killing. But would it not be more unpleasant to see these giants of the wildlife family—the largest land animals on Earth today—be wiped off the face of the planet for all times? Think about that!

We still remember and celebrate the lives of mammoths in museum exhibits and programs, television shows, books and movies. In these ways, mammoths still live in the hearts and minds of people all over the world. Long live the mammoths.

THE END

LONG LIVE BIG M!

FURTHER READING

Agusti, Jordi and Anton, Mauricio. (2005). *Mammoths, Saber Tooths and Hominids—65 Million Years of Mammalian Evolution in Europe.* New York, NY: Columbia University Press.

Cohen, Claudine. (2002). *The Fate of the Mammoth: Fossils, Myths and History.* Chicago, IL: University of Chicago Press.

Goecke, Michael P. (2004). *American Mastodon.* Edina, MN: Abdo Publishing Co.

Grant, Eleanor, Director. (2011). *Ice Age Death Trap: Uncovering Mammoths, Mastodons, and other Vanishing Beasts.* (Video). PBS

Hehner, Barbara, and Hallett, Mark. (2001). *Ice Age Mammoth— Will this Ancient Giant Come Back to Life?* New York, NY: Crown Publishing Group.

Lister, Adrian. (2014). *Mammoths and Mastodons of the Ice Age.* Richmond Hill, ON, Canada: Firefly Books.

Shapiro, Beth. (2015). How to Clone a Mammoth. Princeton, NJ: Princeton University Press.

Ukraintseva,Valentina V. (2013). *Mammoths and the Environment.* Cambridge, UK: Cambridge University Press.

PERMISSIONS AND CREDITS

All photos by the author unless otherwise noted.

I would like to thank the City of Moorpark for granting permission to reproduce materials from Abdouch, Curtis D., *The Mammoth of Moorpark: Big M*, the brochure I wrote in 2006.

Image of Southern Mammoth by Jan Mecklenburg, used with permission, City of Moorpark, California.

I am grateful to Jennifer Bassman for her illustrations of **BIG M** and the wild horses, to Pat Ortega for her sketch of the western camel, and to Matt Aquino for the sabertoothed cat sketch, all used with permission.

Thanks to the Santa Barbara Museum of Natural History for allowing me to take photographs of several of the **BIG M** displays, namely her molar and foot bones.

The Cro-Magnon artists in the Font de Gaume cave in southwest France was done by Charles R. Knight in 1920 and is found on Wikipedia.

The painting of the mammoth in the pond is copyright 2001 by Mark Hallett and used with permission.

A very special thanks to the Columbia Gorge Discovery Center and Museum, Executive Director Carolyn Purcell, and to artist Stev H. Ominski for permission to reproduce a significant section of the painting "The Rowena Incident," that appears as the frontispiece of this book. This magnificent 10-foot by 9.5-foot painting was commissioned by the museum and is on permanent exhibit. Copyright 2007.

I'm grateful to Mammoth Moving for permission to use the photo of their moving van and for the care with which they transported **BIG M**.

I thank the University Pennsylvania Mammoth Genome Project for permission to reproduce the photo of the researcher in their lab.

My photo on the back cover was taken while I was on assignment in Istanbul and is by Amy Moen.

Finally, I am very grateful to Sunbelt Publications for permission to reproduce the painting by John Francis of a mammoth with two young that appears on the cover of this book. Credit: *From Fossil Treasures of the Anza-Borrego Desert,* edited by George T. Jefferson and Lowell Lindsay, copyright 2006.

ACKNOWLEDGMENTS

I would like to express my deep appreciation to the following people who were instrumental in the preparation of this book.

Hugh Riley, Assistant City Manager, City of Moorpark, California. Hugh's political and civic-minded instincts clearly saw the potential for scientific integrity and community pride that could result from a paleontological discovery of this significance. Under his leadership, the Moorpark Mammoth Education Project was born. Among its benefits were a media campaign, a stunning full-color portrait of the Moorpark mammoth, mammoth-related product development, a traveling exhibit and educational materials, all based on contributions from private donors and the sustained interest of many different sources.

Mark Roeder, paleontologist and chief excavator of the mammoth specimen in Moorpark, is a good friend. Mark has years of paleontological experience in California and is a respected member of the scientific and education communities. After his work was completed I had the good fortune to become involved with the Moorpark Mammoth Education Project as an educational and interpretive program consultant. I'm also grateful to Mark for contributing some of his field notes and excavation site maps.

I am especially grateful to the artists who prepared the illustrations that brought to life **BIG M** and her contemporaries from those distant days. (See credits.)

Mark Neal prepared the map showing how **BIG M** and her ancestors arrived in California via the land bridge that once linked Siberia and Alaska.

Shelley Cox, laboratory director at the George C. Page Museum of La Brea Discoveries in Los Angeles, California provided valuable information on the mammoth specimens found at the La Brea Tar Pits. I thank her for her assistance.

Gregory Brown, Chief Preparator, Vertebrate Paleontology, at the University of Nebraska State Museum in Lincoln, Nebraska provided a wealth of information on "Archie," one of the Moorpark mammoth's cousins. I also benefited from his insights and our lively and enlightening conversation about elephant taxonomy and systematics.

For Paul Collins, Curator of Vertebrate Zoology and Krista Fahy, Associate Curator of Vertebrate Zoology, my deep appreciation for providing access to the Santa Barbara Museum of Natural History's collection of **Big M's** specimens.

Dr. Steven Rowland in the Department of Geological Science at the University of Nevada, Las Vegas supplied important insights and information on the nature and distribution of southern mammoths.

I am grateful to Craig B. Smith, my editor and publisher, who carried out the mammoth task of encouraging me to get this story written, all the time remaining patient and supportive.

Thanks to Nancy J. Smith for her meticulous copy editing.

Finally, to Her Highness, **BIG M**, the Moorpark mammoth: she could have remained buried, lost and anonymous forever. However, having come to light, if not to life again, she has provided inspiration and livelihood for many. The full measure of her legacy is yet to be realized.

ABOUT THE AUTHOR

Curt Abdouch is a professional naturalist, environmental educator and writer. He is founder and president of *juST-EAMagine*, a private firm that provides educational services and resources for schools, school districts, communities, museums and libraries.

His museum and wildlife conservation work and travel have taken him to many countries throughout the planet and have solidified his affinity for and expertise in exotic places, wildlife and the outdoors. *juST-EAMagine* reflects and fuels these passions. He is the former Administrator of the fascinating George C. Page Museum of La Brea Discoveries in Los Angeles at the world famous La Brea Tar Pits.

A NOTE ABOUT THE FONTS

Century Schoolbook (text) is familiar to many American readers as the first typeface they encountered in school books. It was designed in 1919 by Morris Fuller Benton for the American Type Founders organization, at the request of Ginn and Company, a textbook publisher. They were seeking a type face that would be easy for young readers. Mr. Fuller employed research that indicated what type of letter forms were most quickly identified by young readers.

Elephant (Main titles, front cover). The Elephant font was designed by famous designer Matthew Carter. Elephant and Elephant italic resulted from a re-working of a traditional English extra bold serif style. Originally, Elephant appeared in posters, often alternating from Roman to italic on successive lines. It is known for its eye-catching appeal. What else could you use for a book about an elephant?

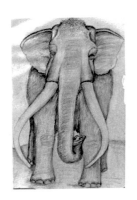

Made in the USA
San Bernardino, CA
27 June 2015